# Sir Cumference and the Great Knight of Angleland

## A Math Adventure

By Cindy Neuschwander

Illustrated by Wayne Geehan

Charlesbridge

Published by Charlesbridge, 85 Main Street, Watertown, MA 02472
(617) 926-0329 • www.charlesbridge.com

Printed by Sung In Printing in Gunpo-Si, Kyonggi-Do, Korea
(hc) 10 9 8 7 6
(sc) 30 29 28 27 26 25

**Library of Congress Cataloging-in-Publication Data**
Neuschwander, Cindy.
Sir Cumference and the great knight of angleland : a math adventure /
by Cindy Neuschwander; illustrated by Wayne Geehan.
p. cm.
Summary: To earn his knighthood, Radius must find and rescue a missing king. His father,
Sir Cumference, and his mother, Lady Di of Ameter, give him a circular medallion
(a protractor) that he uses to find his way through a maze of many angles.
ISBN 978-1-57091-170-5 (reinforced for library use)
ISBN 978-1-57091-169-9 (softcover)
ISBN 978-1-60734-558-9 (ebook)
ISBN 978-1-60734-150-5 (ebook pdf)
1. Geometry—Juvenile literature. [1. Geometry.]
I. Geehan, Wayne ill. II. Title.
QA445.5 .N49 2001
516—dc21
00-011666

*To my son Douglas who already knows all the angles — W.G.*

*For my heavenly Father and for Seth, Andrea, and Tim who know all the angles, too — C.N.*

More than anything, Radius wanted to be a knight. Every day, he practiced riding, sword fighting, and archery. His teacher was the brave, old Sir D'Grees.

One day, Radius's parents, Sir Cumference and Lady Di of Ameter, came to watch his lessons. "Show us what you have learned," they said.

In the riding ring, Radius mounted his horse and Sir D'Grees gave directions. "Knightly right angle — trot!" shouted Sir D'Grees.

Radius rode his horse at a trot to the center of the ring and made an exact right angle turn. It formed a perfect corner.

"Now, double the right angle to make a straight angle!" called out Sir D'Grees. Radius rode at a full gallop straight across the ring. He came to an abrupt stop right in front of his parents.

"Wonderful!" they exclaimed. "You have learned so much."

At supper, Sir D'Grees said, "Radius is the best squire I have ever taught. He is ready to go on a quest."

"He is not old enough," said Sir Cumference, looking worried.

Lady Di smiled. "You were the same age, dear, when you went on your first quest."

Radius sat up straighter. "I am ready, Father," he said. "Please let me go."

Sir Cumference slowly looked at each of them. Finally, he smiled and nodded.

"Hurrah!" shouted Radius, "I will make you proud. But how shall I find someone in need of help?"

"Our neighbor, King Lell, has disappeared," Sir D'Grees answered. "Many have set out to find him, but none has ever returned."

"I will search until I succeed!" promised Radius.

The next morning, Radius made ready to go.

"Remember your knightly right angle, Radius," counseled Sir D'Grees. "It will serve you well."

Sir Cumference and Lady Di gave Radius an old family heirloom — a medallion in the shape of a perfect circle.

"What are these numbers around the edge of the medallion?" Radius asked.

"No one knows," Lady Di answered, "but may it bring you courage on your journey."

Radius bid them farewell and set off.

"I'm on a quest!" he exclaimed gleefully.

Radius rode for many days through the countryside. One day, he came upon a tiny village where all the cottages had rooftops pointed in steep angles.

"What a quaint, little town," thought Radius. "Mother would call it 'cute.'" He asked a villager about King Lell.

"His castle lies beyond the Mountains of Obtuse," said the villager, pointing to the east. "But take heed! There are tales of strange creatures and dangerous labyrinths. No one traveling there has ever returned."

"I hope to be the first," said Radius. "Farewell, and thank you."

Up and down, through the Mountains of Obtuse, Radius rode eastward.

Finally, Radius came upon a walled castle surrounded by a watery moat. He rode cautiously onto the drawbridge. It creaked and groaned with every step.

As he neared the middle, the drawbridge began to crumble. Quickly Radius urged his horse across. Just as they reached the other side, the old drawbridge collapsed into the water with a tremendous splash.

"That was close!" Radius exclaimed. He rode through the high gates of the castle.

In the courtyard, Radius saw a parchment hanging on a door. He took the parchment and read the faded writing.

*Warning, stranger, friend or foe,*
*Dangers wait as forth you go.*
*You must make a Knightly Right,*
*Finding next Big, Straight, and Slight.*
*One wrong turn means lost to all,*
*In a writhing, screaming fall.*
*Find the Right to reach the king,*
*Or you will feel the dragon's sting!*
*The Brothers Zig and Zag*

"What can this mean?" thought Radius. Clutching his medallion for courage, he rode through the doorway into a circular chamber. In the middle of the stone floor, Radius could see a carved circle with a line across its center. All around him, arches led to different rooms.

"Which way should I go?" he wondered aloud. He read from the parchment, "'You must make a Knightly Right.' Sir D'Grees and I practiced many right angle turns."

Just then, something flapped out of the shadows and bumped his arm. "Oof!" grunted Radius as his medallion went flying.

The medallion rolled away and came to a stop on the carved, stone circle. Radius noticed that the number 90 pointed directly toward one of the arches. "Starting at zero on my medallion, if I go to the center and then to the number 90, that forms a right angle. That's the knightly right!" he cried.

Radius swung himself back onto his horse and rode through the arch that was a knightly right, or 90 on the medallion.

The way was dark and damp. Around him, unseen things scuttled in the corners.

By the light of a flickering candle, Radius read the parchment again. "'Finding next Big, Straight, and Slight.'

"What is big?" he wondered. "Could it be something even larger than the knightly right angle?" He thought for a moment. "The Mountains of Obtuse were shaped like big angles," he remembered. As Radius looked around for a way out, spiderwebs caught in his hair and tickling legs brushed against his face.

Ahead, Radius saw several hallways. Each had a circle carved in front of it. "If I hold the medallion over a circle, then the number measures the angle to the hallway," he said. The angle of the first hallway measured only 55 on the medallion.

As Radius measured the angle of each hallway, he found only one that was bigger than a right angle. One angle measured 120 on the medallion.

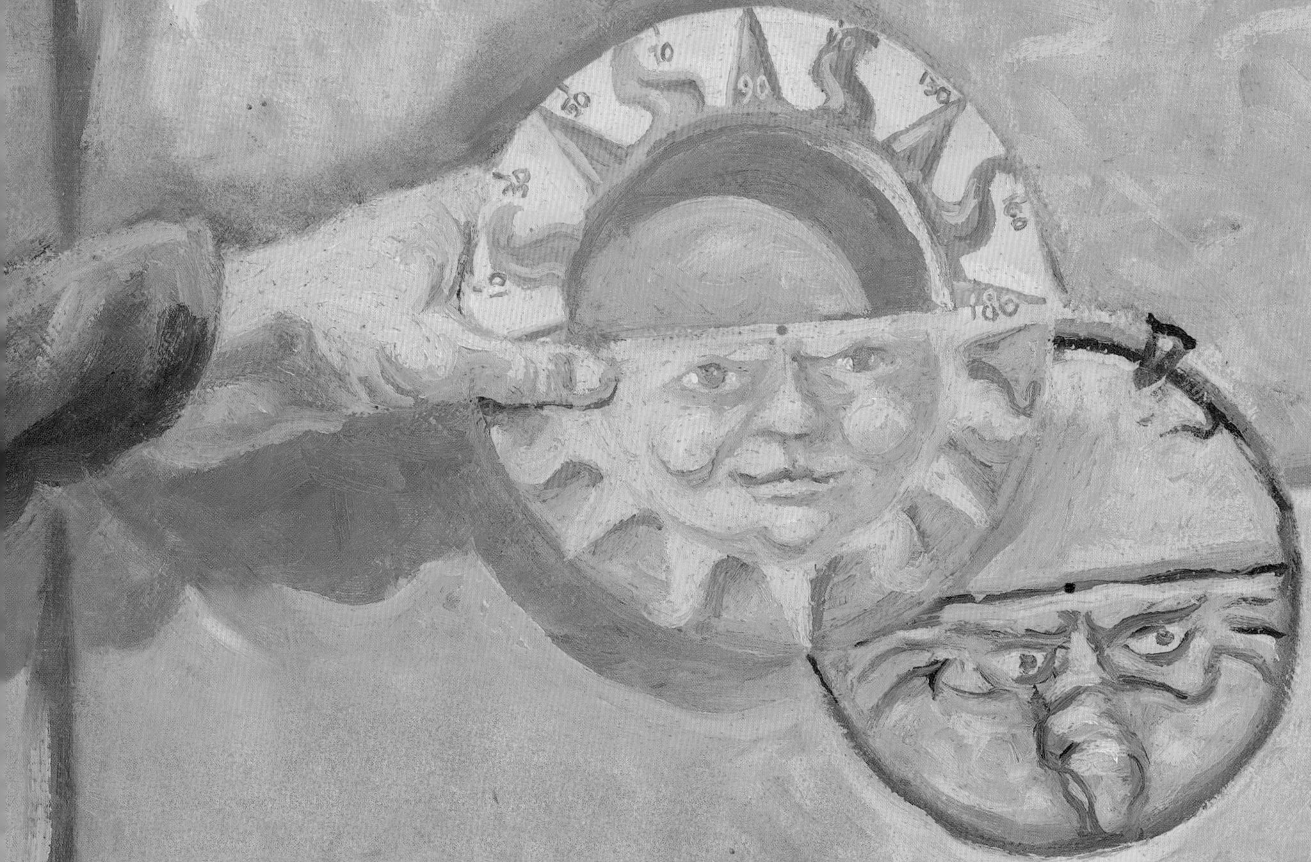

Radius entered that hallway, but it ended at a curving stairway.

Radius dismounted and told his horse to wait. "Stairs are no place for you," he said. "Stay right here. I'll come back as soon as I can."

The stairway down was narrow and steep. "I must be under the castle by now," Radius thought. He noticed that the farther down he went, the hotter it was.

The stairs came to an end at a fiery pit where huge flames leaped up like angry, snapping jaws.

Two bridges spanned the inferno. They both started from the same spot, but they crossed the fire pit at different angles.

"After 'Big,' the parchment reads 'Straight,'" Radius remembered. "That's 180 on my medallion. You can't get an angle straighter than that!" He took a deep breath and ran across the bridge that went straight over the roaring fire.

On the other side, Radius heaved a sigh of relief. He opened a heavy door and entered a dark tunnel. The door clanged shut behind him.

Raspy snuffling came from deep in the darkness. Four glowing eyes appeared and began moving slowly toward him.

Clutching his medallion, Radius hurtled down the tunnel. As he passed the eyes, he brushed against scales that felt like cold chain mail.

Radius ran blindly on, stumbling as the floor started to slope upward. Behind him, heavy thumps echoed in the darkness.

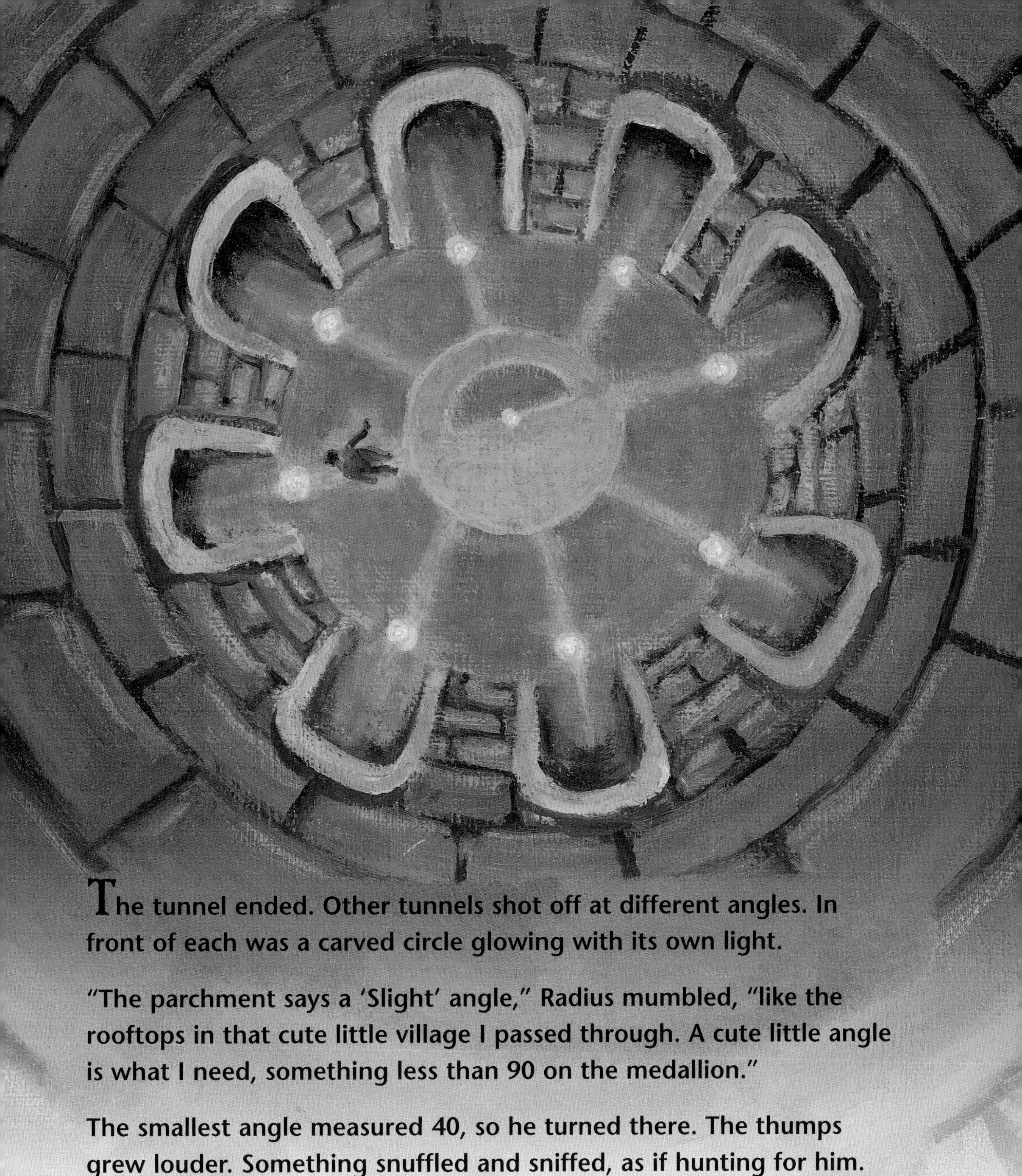

The tunnel ended. Other tunnels shot off at different angles. In front of each was a carved circle glowing with its own light.

"The parchment says a 'Slight' angle," Radius mumbled, "like the rooftops in that cute little village I passed through. A cute little angle is what I need, something less than 90 on the medallion."

The smallest angle measured 40, so he turned there. The thumps grew louder. Something snuffled and sniffed, as if hunting for him.

Radius ran through the darkness. "Next will be the 'Right to reach the king' — another knightly right angle of 90.

"At least the last angle will be easy," he gasped. He was wrong.

In the dim light, he came across four corridors which all seemed to be right angles! Fingers fumbling, he measured quickly with the medallion — 90, 90, 90 — and 90 again!

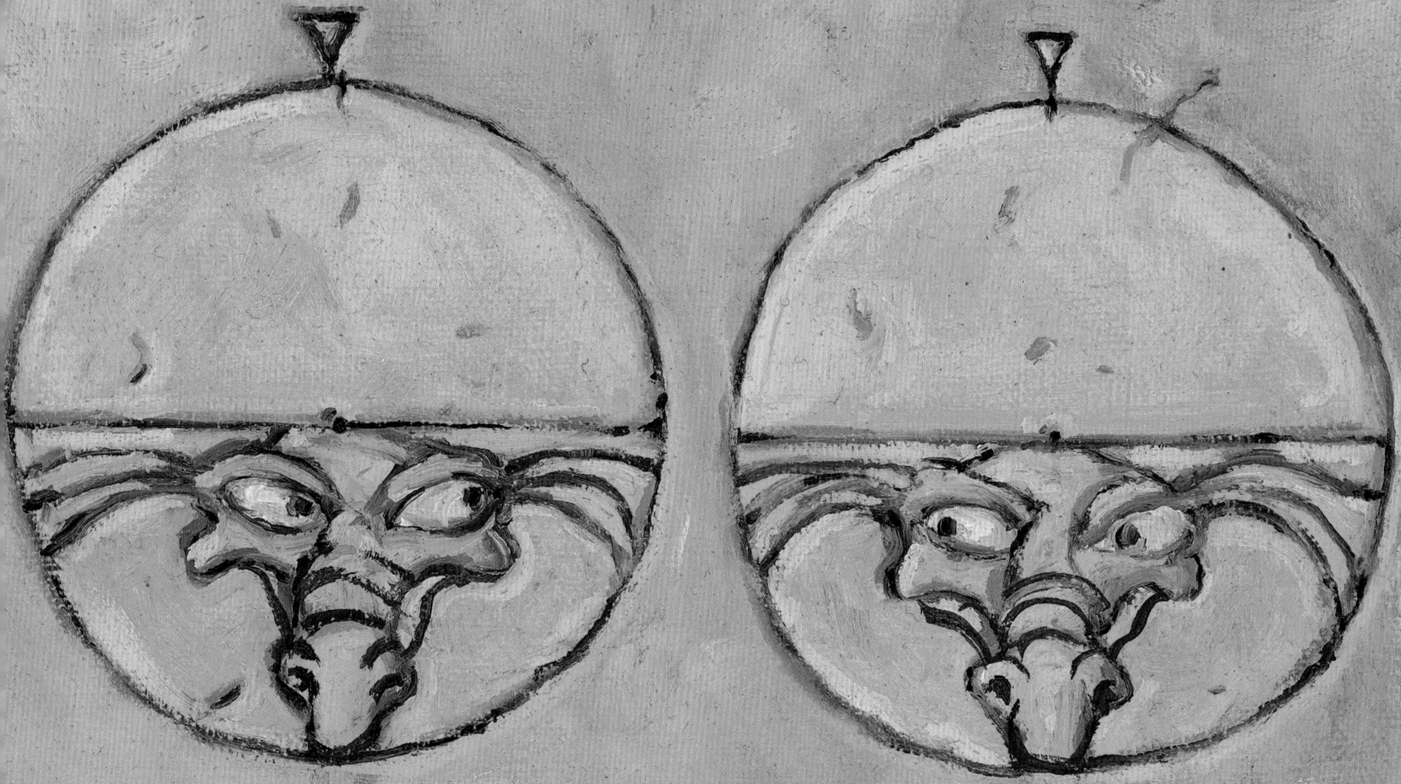

"Slow down," Radius told himself, "and measure once more." He carefully lined up the medallion and read the numbers. The first angle was 93.

"Too big," he said. The next angle was 85. "Too small," he muttered.

The third one was 89. "Almost right," he said.

Then there was a great whooshing sound and thick smoke filled the tunnel.

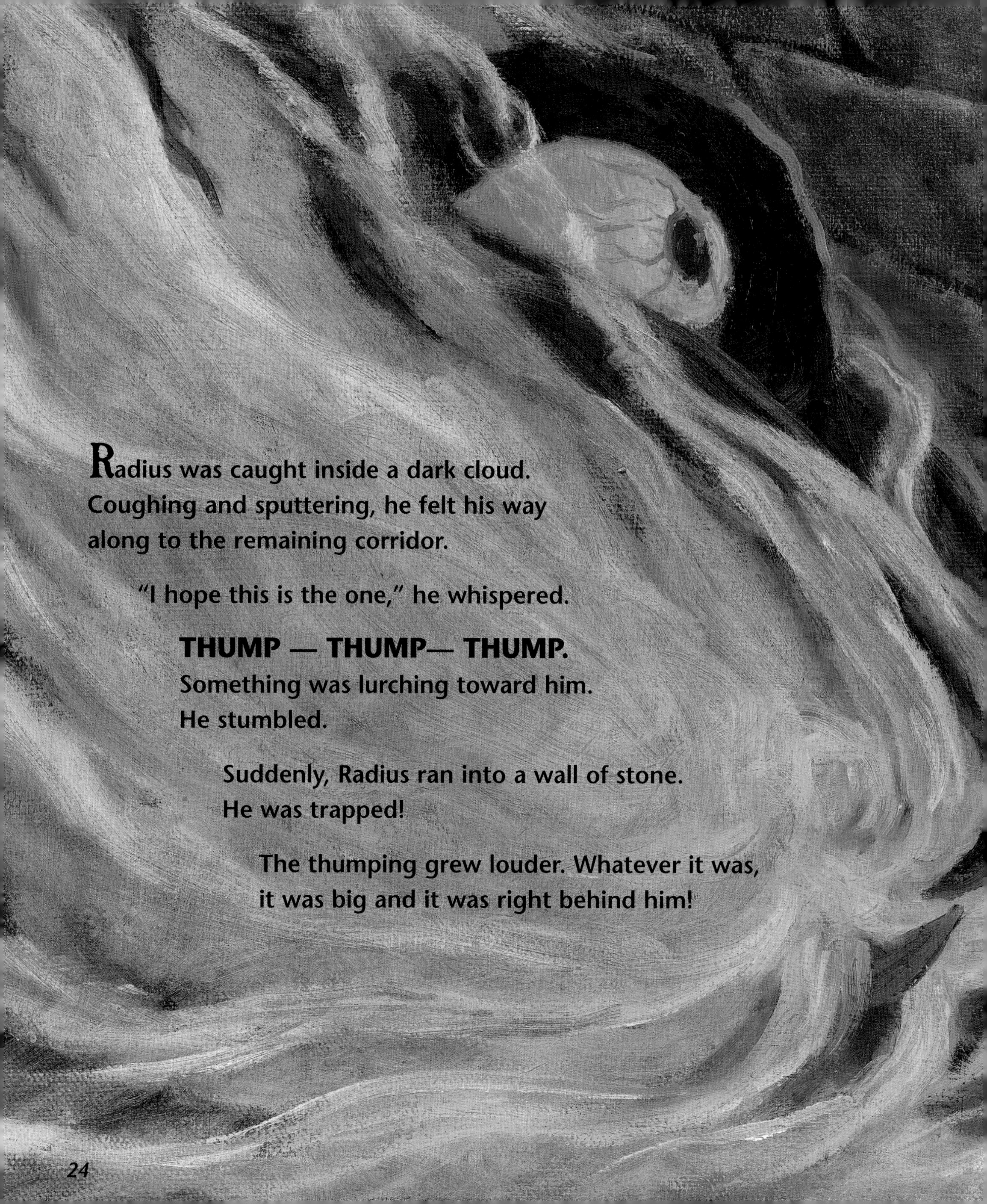

Radius was caught inside a dark cloud. Coughing and sputtering, he felt his way along to the remaining corridor.

"I hope this is the one," he whispered.

**THUMP — THUMP— THUMP.**
Something was lurching toward him. He stumbled.

Suddenly, Radius ran into a wall of stone. He was trapped!

The thumping grew louder. Whatever it was, it was big and it was right behind him!

Radius turned around and stood with his back to the wall. His arm bumped into . . . . a latch . . . . a handle . . . . He pushed with all his strength, and a door swung open.

Brilliant sunshine met his eyes. "Welcome!" a voice bellowed. "Who might you be?"

Radius squinted into the brightness. "I am Radius, son of Sir Cumference and Lady Di of Ameter, and squire to Sir D'Grees. I am searching for King Lell."

"It seems you have found him," chuckled the king, "but how did you do it?"

Radius bowed. "My medallion helped me figure out which paths to take. Knowledge gave me the courage to keep going," he explained. "But there were frightful things in there!"

A whimpering came from behind the door. King Lell opened it wider. Radius jumped back. "Dragons!" he gulped. "A pair of them!"

"They are my loyal pets, the Lell Dragons," explained the king. He scratched their heads. "The poor beasts and I were trapped in the maze by my evil cousins Zig and Zag. But we are free now that you have found the way through the labyrinth.

"Young squire," he continued, "anyone brave enough and smart enough to figure out that maze deserves his knighthood!"

With Radius's medallion, they easily found their way back through the maze. To celebrate King Lell's freedom, invitations were sent to all the neighboring knights and ladies. Sir Cumference, Lady Di of Ameter, and even old Sir D'Grees came. Radius and King Lell went to the moat to greet each group of guests.

When King Lell whistled and called out, "Pair of Lells!" the two dragons stretched across the moat, side by side. They became a living drawbridge for the guests to cross.

Everyone asked Radius how he found his way through the maze. "I discovered the secret of the medallion," Radius said. "The numbers divide a circle into 360 parts. I can use those parts to measure any angle. I call the parts of a circle *degrees* in honor of my teacher, Sir D'Grees."

Radius drew a picture of his medallion and took an arrow from his quiver. "Let's say this arrow points to a hallway. The number shows how many degrees are in the angle.

"A right angle measures 90 degrees. A straight line measures 180 degrees. I call angles bigger than 90 degrees *obtuse* after the Mountains of Obtuse. Angles smaller than 90 I call *acute.* They look like the roofs in a small village I traveled through."

King Lell told Radius to kneel. "For your bravery and intelligence, I knight you Sir Radius!" the king proclaimed.

"From this day forth, let this kingdom be called Angleland. Banners will fly on every castle tower! They shall show knightly right angles of 90 degrees, small acute angles, large obtuse angles, and straight angles of 180 degrees.

"Rise now, great knight of Angleland!"

The crowd cheered, and Radius rose to greet them.

Angleland was the only kingdom to have a castle with a living drawbridge. The cry "Pair of Lells!" brought the two dragons over the moat. They became so famous that today *parallel* means any straight lines side by side, the same distance apart, like the Lell Dragons.

Angleland is still there on very old maps, but today we call it England.